MARK SHANNON

GAWAIN
AND THE
GREEN KNIGHT

ILLUSTRATED BY

DAVID SHANNON

G. P. PUTNAM'S SONS ◾ NEW YORK

For our parents, Martha and Roger

Text copyright © 1994 by Mark Shannon. Illustrations copyright ©1994 by David Shannon.
All rights reserved. This book, or parts thereof, may not be reproduced in any form without
permission in writing from the publisher. G. P. Putnam's Sons, a division of The Putnam & Grosset Group,
200 Madison Avenue, New York, NY 10016. G. P. Putnam's Sons, Reg. U.S. Pat. & Tm. Off.
Published simultaneously in Canada. Printed in Hong Kong by South China Printing Co. (1988) Ltd.
Book designed by Gunta Alexander. Text set in Jenson.
Library of Congress Cataloging-in-Publication Data
Shannon, Mark. Gawain and the Green Knight / by Mark Shannon : illustrated by David Shannon.
p. cm. Summary: Young Gawain proves himself a worthy knight when he accepts the challenge of a
mysterious visitor from the North Country. 1. Gawain (Legendary character)—Juvenile literature.
2. Arthurian romances. [1. Gawain (Legendary character) 2. Folklore—England. 3. Knights and
knighthood—Folklore.] I. Shannon, David. 1959- ill. II. Gawain and the Green Knight. III. Title.
PZ8.1.S495Gaw 1994 398.2—dc20 [E821'.1] 93-13037 CIP AC ISBN 0-399-22446-7
10 9 8 7 6 5 4 3 2 1

Each year at Christmastime, a Yuletide celebration
filled King Arthur's castle with music, feasting and stories.
The Knights of the Round Table told tales of adventures in
the North Country, where strange enchanters put the
knights' courage and virtue to the test. Each tale, it seemed,
grew more wondrous than the one before.

"Tell us, young Gawain," said one knight with a chuckle. "What great deed of *yours* will we tell?"

"Well, I–" Gawain stuttered, for he was the youngest and most inexperienced of the knights.

"I-I-I'll charm the birds right out of the treetops with my-my-my eloquent tongue," interrupted another, and all the knights and ladies at the table laughed.

This was not the first joke they had poked at shy young Gawain. But this time a girl named Caryn cried, "I think Gawain will one day rival the best of you!" She spoke with such emotion that the company laughed again. But they were stopped by a voice as big as summer thunder.

"Pardon me, good King," it boomed.

All heads turned at once toward the entranceway. There stood the oddest-looking man anyone had ever seen. Taller than the tallest of knights, with legs broad as oaks, he was green from head to toe. Only the gold trim on his tunic broke the enchanted expanse, and his eyes, which glowed red as burning coals.

"Brave and noble Knights of the Round Table," the Green Knight proclaimed. "I come proposing a little Yuletide game, a test of your courage. One of you may launch an unhindered blow of this axe at my neck. However, should I manage to survive, I must be allowed a swing in return. And because I am a sporting man, my fellow player may have a year and a day's time before I take up the blade."

Gawain felt his blood stir. This is my chance, he thought. He stepped forward. "I'll do it!" he said, then more loudly, "I accept the challenge!"

The Green Knight's laughter rushed through the hall like a spring wind galloping through trees.

"Good luck, lad," the Green Knight said, still chuckling. His breath smelled sweet and rotten like cut grass left too long in the corner of a barn. Then he knelt down on all fours and said, "She's all yours, young knight," and he tapped the back of his exposed neck.

Gawain stole a glance at Caryn. Then he took a deep breath, swung the glinting blade high into the air and brought it hurtling back down. The axe clanged on the stone floor and the Green Knight's hairy head went twisting and flying from his body.

"Oh my goodness," Gawain whispered as the head rolled across the floor. But the silence of the crowd quickly gave way to an astonished gasp. For the Green Knight was standing up! Then he tromped confidently over to his head, plucked it up by the hair, and held it aloft like a lantern.

"And now, young Gawain," spoke the head. "As we agreed, you have one year and a day until we meet for my turn with the blade. You will find me in the North Country, where I am known as the Knight of the Green Chapel. Farewell." And with that he grabbed his axe and passed back under the stone arch of the door, his deep laughter echoing through the hall behind him.

In the days and months that followed, Gawain and
Caryn spent more and more time together. But before they
knew it, winter had come again. Soon the time approached for
Gawain to keep his promised rendezvous with the Knight of
the Green Chapel.

The evening before he was to leave, Gawain and Caryn
climbed high up in a castle tower to watch the snow falling
over the hills. The light was blue and all the world seemed to
be silent.

"I have something for you, Gawain," Caryn said then.
And from inside her cloak she produced a silk sash woven with
intricate pictures.

"All year long, in secret, I have been weaving this. Take it
with you on your journey as a keepsake, for good luck." And
she handed him the sash.

As bravely as he could, Gawain said, "Until I return,
I will never take it off. I promise."

The next day, as he had agreed, Gawain prepared to go in search of the Green Chapel. The Knights of the Round Table dressed him in the finest armor and praised his courage and wished him good fortune. For, despite their jokes, Gawain was much loved by the knights. Then he rode into the cold winter morning.

Day after day Gawain spurred his horse, Gringolet,
onward, and night after night he shivered in the icy cold.
But nowhere did he find a single soul who could direct him
to the Green Chapel. Soon the young knight left the farm
country and its haylofts behind. Cragged mountains rose up
like the teeth of wolves. But still, no one had heard of the
Green Knight.

Finally, as Yuletide drew close, Gawain caught sight of a glorious castle rising out of the mists before him on a high plateau.

Thanking his good fortune, Gawain pulled up at the castle gates and shouted, "I am a knight of King Arthur's Round Table seeking the Green Chapel. Can you help me?"

Presently the huge wooden doors creaked open. "Well hello, traveling knight," said the big, cheerful man who came out to greet him. "I am Sir Bertilak. I would be glad to help you. But first you must stay the night with my wife and me for our Yuletide feast. For we love visitors from the South." Then he laughed a good-natured laugh.

So Gawain was given a warm bath and fresh clothing.
At dinner he was seated in a place of honor between Sir
Bertilak and his wife. Never had he tasted such delicious
spices, or been entertained by someone as charming as Lady
Bertilak. Her laughter was as clear as music, and when she
spoke, her hands moved like birds through the air.

Finally all the castle had gone to sleep, but Gawain tossed and turned in the huge bed of the castle guest chamber, wondering if this might be his last night on earth. After some time, he heard a light knock on the door. It inched open and Lady Bertilak entered. Her long hair fell loose, almost to her waist, and her eyes glowed with a light so pale and enchanting that Gawain wondered if he might be dreaming.

"The Green Knight," the Lady whispered, approaching Gawain, "is a most deadly foe, indeed. But I know a way you might be spared." As she moved closer, her hair shone as though it were spun from moonlight.

"Trade me your sash," she continued, "for this one." From out of her robe, she pulled a band of crimson silk. "It is a magical sash, Gawain. It will protect you from the Green Knight's axe, and spare your life."

The dark folds of the sash seemed to stretch and wind before Gawain like a path through a vast wood. But in his mind's eye, Caryn appeared and his heart rose up. "No," he said. "Your offer is kind. But if I do indeed lose my life, it will be with this sash I now wear tied around my waist. I have made my promise."

"So be it then," Lady Bertilak said. "Good luck, young Gawain." Then she walked toward the door. To the weary knight it seemed as though she had vanished into the first rays of dawn. Gray light crept into the chamber and it was morning.

And so, Gawain soon found himself riding into the valley that held the Green Knight and his chapel. A screeching, grinding sound tore the air, and sparks flew like red rain through the clear morning. The Green Knight was sharpening his axe.

"Welcome, lad!" shouted the knight to Gawain. His laughter bounced and crackled down the narrow valley. With as much courage as he could muster, Gawain knelt to receive the fearsome knight's blow. He thought of Caryn and of all the pictures on the sash as the axe came hurtling down.

Gawain waited a moment and then a moment more. He felt a warm drop of blood trickle down his neck. But his head was still on his shoulders!

He stood up and boldly drew his long sword. But the Green Knight just smiled down at him. "Now don't go and spoil our good sport with that sword of yours, Sir Gawain," the Green Knight said. Then he held out his hand. Astonished, Gawain nevertheless thrust his sword back into its sheath and, as was the old custom, clasped the Green Knight's wrist.

"Consider yourself a true champion in our little game!" the Green Knight continued. "You proved your knightly passion when you accepted our challenge, and your honesty and courage when you kept your promised rendezvous. And, most important of all–" Then a voice sounded from the depths of the Green Chapel.

"Most important of all," said Lady Bertilak, who was walking out now to join the Green Knight, "you were true to the mysteries of your own heart." Then the Green Knight let loose a loud laugh and his tangled hair glowed red as a sunset. A moment later, there before Gawain's wide eyes stood Sir Bertilak.

"You have quite a tale to tell at the Round Table now, lad, eh?" he said, and laughed again. "And that nick on your neck, consider it a little souvenir of the North Country."

"Farewell then," Gawain said warmly. He mounted his horse and waved good-bye in the bright winter morning. Then he turned and spurred Gringolet out of the valley, back toward Caryn, King Arthur and home.